D0549499

. . . . . WHAT'S AT ISSUE? . .

ANIMAL RIGHTS?

Paul Wignall

HAMILTON COLLEGE
R06387L0777

Heinemann
LIBRARY

HAMILTON COLLEGE LIBRARY

www.heinemann.co.uk
Visit our website to find out more information about **Heinemann Library** books.

To order:
 Phone 44 (0) 1865 888066
Send a fax to 44 (0) 1865 314091
Visit the Heinemann Bookshop at www.heinemann.co.uk to browse our catalogue
and order online.

First published in Great Britain by Heinemann Library, Halley Court, Jordan Hill, Oxford
OX2 8EJ, a division of Reed Educational and Professional Publishing Ltd. Heinemann is a
registered trademark of Reed Educational & Professional Publishing Limited.

OXFORD   MELBOURNE   AUCKLAND   JOHANNESBURG   BLANTYRE
GABORONE   IBADAN   PORTSMOUTH NH (USA)   CHICAGO

© Reed Educational and Professional Publishing Ltd 2001
The moral right of the proprietor has been asserted.

All rights reserved. No part of this publication may be reproduced, stored in a retrieval system, or
transmitted in any form or by any means, electronic, mechanical, photocopying, recording, or
otherwise without either the prior written permission of the Publishers or a licence permitting
restricted copying in the United Kingdom issued by the Copyright Licensing Agency Ltd,
90 Tottenham Court Road, London W1P 0LP.

Designed by Tinstar Design (www.tinstar.co.uk)
Originated by Ambassador Litho Ltd
Printed in Hong Kong/China

ISBN 0 431 03543 1   (hardback)   ISBN 0 431 03550 4   (paperback)
04 03 02 01   05 04 03 02 01
10 9 8 7 6 5 4 3 2 1   10 9 8 7 6 5 4 3 2 1

British Library Cataloguing in Publication Data
Wignall, Paul
        Animal rights. – (What's at issue?)
        1. Animal Rights – Juvenile literature
        I. Title
        179.3

Acknowledgements
The Publishers would like to thank the following for permission to reproduce photographs:
Bodliean Library: p16; Bridgeman Art Library: pp4, 10, 14, 18, 23, 27, 32, 35, Christieís p26;
Chris Oxlade: p34; Corbis: p6, Hulton-Deutsch p22, p25, Bettman p30, Neil Preston p31,
Dewitt Jones p34, Bob Rowan p38, Tom Brakefield p39, John Periam p40; Heinemann: pp5, 12;
The Kobal Collection: p9; NASA: 43; Rex Features: p13, 28, 29, 33, Edward Hirst, Jill Phipps p20,
Nils Jorgensen p24; RSPCA: p36; The Stock Market: p7; Tony Stone Images: Manoj Shah p8,
Will & Deni McIntyre p15, Zigy Kaluzny p17, Gary John Norman p19.

Cover photograph: Tony Stone Images (Gary John Norman).

Our thanks to Julie Turner (School Counsellor, Banbury School, Oxfordshire) for her comments
in the preparation of this book.

Every effort has been made to contact copyright holders of any material reproduced in this book.
Any omissions will be rectified in subsequent printings if notice is given to the Publisher.

Any words appearing in the text in bold, **like this**, are explained in the Glossary.

Contents

Introduction

Human beings share the planet earth with many other animals. The aim of this book is to look at some of the ways humans and animals live together. How should we treat animals? Is it right to kill and eat them for food? Is it right to train them to perform, or to kill them for sport? Do animals have the same sort of 'rights' – to protection and care – as humans? In this book we will see how people have answered these questions in different ways and you will have a chance to answer the questions for yourself.

The diversity of life

Human beings are one of an estimated 1.4 million known species of living things that make up the rich variety of life on our planet. There are more than 4000 different species of mammals (of which human beings are one), over 9000 species of birds and at least 1,000,000 known species of insects, including over 20,000 ants. In England alone there are more than 13,000 different insects, while throughout the world there are probably tens of millions of species of living things still waiting to be discovered.

Since the beginning of life on Earth, species have evolved to live successfully in particular environments. Every corner of our planet, from the tropical rainforests to the arctic icecaps, from town streets to the beds of the deepest seas, has its own distinctive life forms, specially adapted to survive and flourish.

Detail from *Peaceable Kingdom* by Edward Hicks.

Interdependence

The rich diversity of life creates **interdependence**. There is what biologists call a **symbiotic** relationship between different living things and between them and their environment. As some species disappear, so others are endangered. The environment in which they live may then change, making it in turn more hostile to those that are left.

Because species evolve to live in particular environments, it is always possible they will die out when the environment changes. The spectacular ending of the age of the dinosaurs is the best-known example, but the extinction of species is never-ending. Many biologists and environmentalists are concerned that the changes we make to the world around us – such as industrial pollution or the felling of the rainforests – have speeded up the rate of extinction until it may threaten the whole of life.

Biodiversity

Anxiety about human involvement in this reduction of what environmentalists call **biodiversity**, has led to calls for greater respect for the world around us. We are asked to value its diversity and to do all that we can to protect it. But this has to be set alongside the need for human beings to survive and flourish. For example, human beings make much use of timber. But if the felling of trees leads to the extinction of some species of birds, should we stop this practice in order to preserve the birds' habitat, or should we go on meeting human needs and accept the extinctions as part of the 'natural' order of things?

Human beings are just one species among many millions on Earth, but we have the greatest responsibility because we can make decisions like these. Throughout this book, we will see that animal rights are in the end about the way we as human beings take responsible decisions for ourselves and the great diversity of life with which we share our planet.

> People should just get on with their own lives. Why should we worry about animals?

> We all live on the same planet – we need each other.

FACT

● *Humans evolved in Africa millions of years ago. As they did so they fitted successfully into the existing environment, living alongside other species. Humans moved out of Africa into Europe and Asia, then on to America and Australia. In these new environments, they competed with animals and birds for food and shelter, for example. In fact, the movement of humans across the world coincides closely with the extinction of species of animals and birds: from about 30,000 years ago in Australia, about 10,000 years ago in North America, but only from about 2000 years ago in the Pacific islands. The extinctions are now happening at a faster rate than ever. The reduction of the rainforests alone is estimated to cause the disappearance of seventy-four species every day - three every hour.*

Human rights – and responsibilities

The American Declaration of Independence, the first ever statement of human rights, published in 1776, said that 'all men are created equal, that they are endowed with certain inalienable rights, that among these are Life, Liberty, and the pursuit of Happiness'. Today we are used to saying that people have certain basic rights, but in 1776 this was quite a new idea.

Rights and responsibilities

Human rights are also about human responsibilities. Our right to equal treatment has to be balanced by our responsibility to treat other people as equals. At first, such rights and responsibilities were in practice limited to small groups. The American declaration did not prevent the appalling treatment of native Americans, for instance, who were systematically removed from their lands and even killed. However, it was a seed that would lead eventually to a great flowering of justice in the **emancipation** of slaves, the **civil rights movement** and the modern belief that **discrimination** on the grounds of sex, race, or religion, is unacceptable.

The first words of the American Declaration of Independence (4th July 1776). Can animals share in 'rights' like these?

> ### FACT
>
> ● *Statements of human rights reached their most universal form in the words of the United Nations Declaration of Human Rights of 1948: 'The inherent dignity and the equal rights of all members of the human family is the foundation of freedom, justice and peace in the world'.*

Animal rights?

Does this belief in equality, freedom and the 'right' to be treated in certain ways include animals as well? Do animals also have 'inherent dignity' and 'certain inalienable rights to Life, Liberty and the pursuit of Happiness'? This is the fundamental issue behind the debate about animal rights.

IN CONGRESS, JULY 4, 1776.

The unanimous Declaration of the thirteen united States of America

'Rights' are about shared responsibilities, but do animals have them? We might have responsibilities towards animals, but do they have responsibilities to each other, or to people? Human rights are **moral** matters – conscious decisions we take about how we live together and how we behave towards one another. Can animals make decisions like that? No animal could actually read or understand

Pets can be very important to their human carers.

a 'declaration of animal rights'. No animal could tell you what its 'rights' are. And no animal could take you to court for violating its 'rights'. So is the idea of animal rights really about how we think people should behave towards animals? Are animals interested in animal rights?

Animal consciousness

The great diversity of life on our planet ranges from tiny bacteria to massive elephants, from single-celled creatures to complex human beings. All life reacts to external **stimuli**, whether it is a speck of plankton in the sea moving towards sunlight, or you and I moving towards the smell of food when we are hungry.

What is consciousness?

Consciousness is more than the ability to react to a stimulus. It means being aware of the world around us and communicating that awareness. We can talk about the world in which we live, make plans, observe and reflect. We try to bring about pleasurable experiences (we can cook our own dinner when we are hungry, not just wait for the smell of food). We try to foresee and avoid painful experiences.

If we think of all species as an unbroken chain of life, with human beings at one end, fully conscious of the world (after all, not even dolphins write books on animal rights), then how far back along the chain does consciousness extend?

Chimpanzees are humans' closest relatives, and can do many things we do. But can they understand what they are doing?

Research findings

Chimpanzees are our closest living non-human relatives and they have a richly developed consciousness. Those who work closely with chimpanzees say that they experience just about every emotion we do. They can use tools, think ahead, and take care of one another. At Washington University in the United States, a chimpanzee called Washoe has learned American Sign Language, uses it to communicate with humans, and has even taught it to another chimpanzee, Loulis. Researchers also claim that other creatures, such as gorillas, whales and dolphins are more like us than we sometimes think. If it is true that some other species have a capacity for consciousness not far from that of human beings, then maybe we are justified in offering them a share in a declaration of rights, human and animal.

The same as us?

Although people may wish to protect all living species in order to keep our planet in balance, most only want to give animals who have some form of consciousness a 'right' to freedom from cruelty or torture. We may be repelled when we see anyone pulling the legs off a spider or chopping up a worm, but we are more likely to think 'people shouldn't be cruel' than 'worms have rights'. Even if some animal species are more conscious of the world around them than others, this does not necessarily mean they 'feel' or 'think' in the same way that we do.

'EXACTLY LIKE US'?

Anthropomorphism is the mistaken assumption that animals have exactly the same feelings as humans. Many stories use animal characters as though they were human – *Wind in the Willows*, for instance, or *Babe*, or *Animal Farm* – but that does not mean that toads and rats, pigs or horses are really like humans. Assuming that animals are 'exactly like us' is neither kind to animals nor realistic about humans. It can lead not only to the cruelty of feeding too much chocolate to dogs, but also to treating human beings with callous brutality.

Stories that make animals behave like humans can distort our understanding of real animals. This is the cowardly lion from *The Wizard of Oz*.

The animal rights movement – its roots

People have been concerned about human rights for little more than 200 years, although some religious groups, such as the Jains, have always believed that all living creatures should be treated with respect. In fact, the United Kingdom passed laws to protect animals from abuse before there were any laws to protect children. The Society for the Prevention of Cruelty to Animals was founded in 1824 to find and punish people deliberately ill-treating animals.

Henry Salt

The first book on animal rights was written by Englishman Henry Salt in 1892. Salt's argument is based on two different ideas. First, he believed that we are not designed to eat meat. This was not a new idea. More than 100 years earlier, the French thinker Jean-Jacques Rousseau had argued that human teeth and intestines were best suited to eating and digesting fruit and vegetables, and that this should be our natural diet.

Second, Salt linked Rousseau's belief to another great 19th century idea – Charles Darwin's **theory of evolution**. Salt thought that much human treatment of animals – and especially our love of eating them – was evil. He said it was an evil based on the assumption that 'there is a gulf, an impassable barrier, between man and the animals'. As long as we could

persuade ourselves that we were different from other living creatures, we did not have to worry about how we treated them. But, Darwin having shown how 'higher species' such as humans have evolved from the 'lower species', we should accept what Salt called 'their numberless points of kinship with mankind'.

Henry Salt believed that animals have the right to be free to live their own lives and we have responsibilities to treat them compassionately and justly. He wrote in his book that 'no human being is justified as regarding any animal whatsoever as a meaningless automaton, to be worked, or tortured, or eaten, as the case may be, for the mere object of satisfying the wants or whims of mankind.' In other words, animals are to be valued for what they are, not for what we can do with them.

Back to nature

Henry Salt's ideas supported **vegetarianism**, the belief that for good health humans should not eat meat. Early in the 20th century, groups of people all over Europe, especially in southern Germany and Switzerland, began to live simple lives together, going 'back to nature'. They were usually vegetarian and committed to what we would now call **Green** or **environmentally friendly** values. There is an important link between animal rights and the search for simple, sustainable life styles.

Jean-Jacques Rousseau – an 18th century Frenchman whose ideas about human rights have been influential for animal rights activists as well as vegetarians.

Was Henry Salt right?

The animal rights movement started from two main ideas: that human beings are not made to eat meat, and that we have a moral duty to treat animals as 'like us' – that we should behave towards them just as we would behave towards other human beings. But some people do not agree with either of these ideas.

First, some people say, it is a matter of historical and biological fact that humans have always eaten meat, and have evolved as meat-eaters. Early humans are sometimes described as 'hunter-gatherers' – people who hunted animals for food as well as gathering fruits, seeds or nuts to eat. Are we actually different today?

Second, are animals really as 'like us' as other human beings are? This is a complex problem but many people would argue that animals are not 'like' humans at all, although this doesn't mean we shouldn't treat them well and with compassion. In fact, the argument goes, we should treat animals with respect precisely because they are different from us; the need to maintain the diversity of life on our planet is the basis for the way we treat other species.

SALT'S INFLUENCE

The full title of Salt's book was *Animal Rights in Relation to Social Progress*. He wanted to persuade people that refusing to kill and eat animals was the mark of a fully civilized society. The great Indian advocate of non-violent protest, Mahatma Gandhi, said that he learned much about the way humans should treat one another from Salt's book.

The animal liberation movement

During the 1970s two developments thrust animal rights issues back to the centre of the stage. First was the growing awareness that industrial society was a major cause of pollution. Campaigners began to protest about the poisoning of the environment – acid rain destroying forests; radiation and gases released into the atmosphere; and chemicals added to food. While the protests were generally peaceful, they could involve large-scale resistance to the authorities. The protesters also emphasized connections between humans and other species. Animals, they said, just like us, have the right not to have their habitats destroyed.

Liberation

The early declarations of human rights were not just bright ideas, they were calls for freedom. Since Jean-Jacques Rousseau's assertion in 1762 that 'Man was born free, and everywhere he is in chains', human rights has always been linked with the struggle to free people from **oppression**. Since the early 1970s, people have argued that the same is true for animals.

Animal liberation

In 1975 the philosopher Peter Singer wrote a book called *Animal Liberation*. In the book he argues that human attitudes to non-human animals amount to a form of tyranny. Humans, he claims, inflict pain and suffering on animals which is oppressive and wrong, and must stop.

Both Henry Salt and Peter Singer thought that what they had to say was so obviously true that everyone would agree with them, once the oppression was revealed and the wrongs exposed. They also shared the view that the lives of human and non-human animals are of equal value. Where they differed was, first, in the way they argued their case and, second, in what they thought should happen next.

Animals can't fight for themselves – we need to fight for them.

But can it ever be right to cause damage, or to injure people, when we're making a protest?

Peter Singer does not believe that animals have rights, but he does believe we should treat them well. Can we ever justify causing pain to animals – by experimenting on them, killing them for food, or putting them in zoos? Can something that is good for humans, such as a new treatment for cancer, ever be discovered at the expense of the suffering of countless mice injected with substances that cause cancer?

Violent protest

Many liberation movements (such as the struggle against **apartheid** in South Africa) have wavered between peaceful protest and violent action. Animal liberationists have been similarly divided. Peaceful campaigning has brought about changes in the way animals are treated. But some campaigning has been violent. In Britain, in 1982, the Animal Rights Militia sent a letter bomb to the prime minister of the time, Margaret Thatcher. In 1988, the Animal Rights Front firebombed and destroyed a store in Plymouth involved in the fur trade.

Anger at the trade in animal skins, and the use of furs in the fashion industry, was behind attacks on shops by the Animal Rights Front.

Animal experiments – what's been happening?

Scientific experimentation using animals is sometimes called **vivisection**. These experiments have a long history and were one of the first focuses of opposition by animal rights activists.

An Experiment on a Bird in an Air Pump (1768). A painting by Joseph Wright. The artist shows a range of emotions – from the detached scientific view of the man in the centre, to the distress of the children on the right.

Cosmetics research

For many years, animals have been used to test the ingredients of soaps, perfumes and other toiletries, as well as foods and household goods, to discover whether they are likely to be harmful to humans. In **Draize** tests, substances are dripped into rabbits' eyes to see how much irritation is caused. The rabbits are held in special pens so they cannot move, or rub their eyes. In other tests, animals breathe fumes or have their bodies sprayed to see if their skin blisters. Although many of these tests have now been stopped, as recently as ten years ago over 280,000 animals in the United Kingdom alone were subjected to tests in one year.

Public campaigning, including most famously the efforts of The Body Shop, has, since the mid-1980s, reduced animal testing in this area. Many manufacturers advertise their goods as 'not tested on animals'. But the level of monitoring is not always good, and if you want to use products not tested on animals, you need to look at the labels very carefully.

Drugs research

Animals are used to develop new drugs and to test how safe they are. These tests may help in the development of life-saving treatments, for humans or animals, but many simply add another product to an already overcrowded and competitive market. Animals are also tested to see how addictive a drug is. For example, monkeys were taught to take doses of cocaine until they died, while beagles were used to observe the painful withdrawal symptoms from **tranquillizers** such as valium.

THE LD50 TEST

Tests for the safety of cosmetics, household goods or drugs often use the LD50 method. LD50 stands for 'lethal dose 50 per cent': how much of a substance will kill half the animals being studied. The whole group of animals is poisoned and before half of them die, all of them will be in great distress. In the United States alone, several million animals a year are subjected to LD50 tests.

Psychological testing and dissection

Researchers have also used animals to test their reaction to stress or their ability to 'solve problems'. For example, they have looked at what happens when animals are subjected to intense heat, or deprived of sleep, or how rats can find their way round mazes to get food.

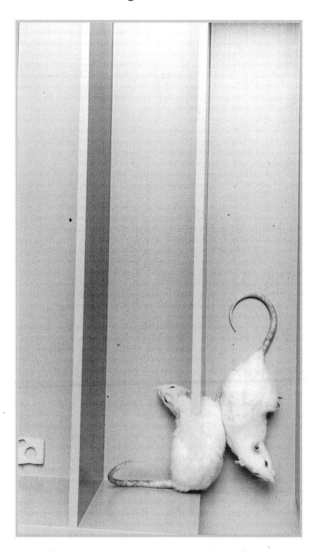

Rats in a maze. Do experiments like this contribute anything to human health, happiness or understanding?

Until recently all students of biology, even in school, learned about animals by dissecting them. After many protests, it was finally agreed that such experiments were not essential and biology students are no longer required to dissect animals.

Animal experiments – should they be happening?

This illustration of an experiment by Claude Bernard in which 'rabbits were roasted alive' comes from Frances Power Cobbe's book *Light in Dark Places* (1885), an early attempt to expose cruel animal experiments.

will not necessarily tell us anything about the effects on humans. So one argument against animal experimentation is the practical one that it is not much use to researchers anyway.

But there are other **moral** arguments against animal experimentation, which say not only that we need not, but also that we should not, do it.

Are they any use?

Most animal experiments tell us little we did not know already. Why poison animals with weedkiller when we know weedkiller is poisonous? Of course one reason may be that researchers are trying to find something to counteract the poison. But researchers have also learned that what affects one species – monkeys – does not necessarily affect another – mice – in the same way. The results of tests on animals

Should we do it?

There are three main lines of argument against using animals for experimentation:
1 Animals should be treated with respect, not for what we can get out of them.
2 Animal experiments cause far more suffering than the benefits to humans could possibly warrant.
3 Animal experiments are a sign of our misguided attitude to nature.

What do you think?

Researchers are continually looking for ways of taking away human or animal pain, or understanding the complexities of life. It is hard to argue that these are not good aims. But, on the other hand, those who argue against animal experiments say we should respect other creatures, let them be themselves and not make them suffer pain. Those seem good aims too. But are there ever times when it is right to use animals in experiments? Or is it always wrong to use animals in this way? What do you think?

ANIMAL RIGHTS

- Henry Salt believed that animals should be treated with the same compassion and justice we show to other people. If it is wrong to make humans suffer, then it is wrong to inflict pain on animals.

- Tom Regan, in his book *The Case for Animal Rights* (1984), has argued that neither people nor animals should be harmed either for our pleasure or for what we can get from them, whether food or information. Animals are precious in themselves, not objects to meet our own needs.

ANIMAL LIBERATION

Peter Singer says that medical research accounted for less than 5 per cent of the falling death-rate in the 20th century (the rest being the result of social and hygiene changes). Only a small portion of this medical research involved experiments on animals, though this involved many millions of such animals as dogs, monkeys and mice. He concludes that the amount of suffering caused to animals far outweighed the experiments' use in prolonging human life.

ANIMALS SHOULD BE THEMSELVES

Stephen Clark, in a book called *The Moral Status of Animals*, argues that animals, just like humans, have the right to 'be themselves' – to fulfil their real potential. Experiments on animals stop them being themselves. We treat them as less important than us, when we should understand that they are just different. Animal experimentation is one way we dominate other living things, a sign of our misguided attitude to nature.

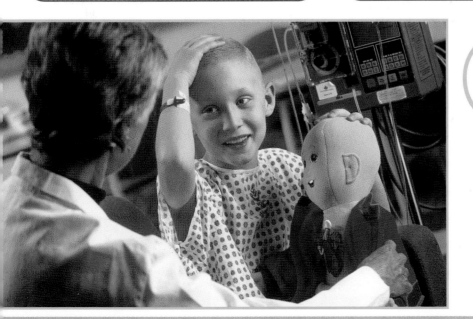

It is thought that four out of ten people are at risk of developing cancer during their lifetime. Animal experiments may help us to find a cure, but is it worth it?

Farming and breeding

The history of agriculture is the history of human relationships with animals. Thousands of years ago, farmers took wild cattle and trained them to pull ploughs and carts. Other originally wild animals – sheep, pigs, chickens, ducks and geese, for instance – have also been **domesticated**, and carefully bred to provide food. Dogs are bred and trained to help protect and manage farm animals. Domesticated animals have been crucial to the growth of human civilization.

Intensive farming and animal rights

As the population has grown, so has the need to provide food as efficiently and cheaply as possible. In the last 50 years, this has led to much more **intensive farming**. In the drive for high output and low cost, farms have taken on many of the characteristics of other industries.

Four areas of agriculture and the food industry concern animal rights activists:
1. The breeding of animals to meet the demands of food manufacturers and customers.
2. The treatment of animals at the farms.
3. The way in which animals are transported from farm to factory.
4. The methods used in killing animals before they are turned into the food you and I can buy and eat.

Ploughing with harnessed oxen, Egypt. The use of animals by humans goes back to the earliest of civilizations.

Genetic modification

The cattle, sheep and dogs we see today are the result of generations of careful breeding. Until quite recently, no one knew the biological basis for this, but as we understand how the '**genetic code**' that affects all life works, it is possible to be much more precise in the changes we can make. For example, scientists are working to identify genes that resist disease. Introducing these into animals

Hens in a battery cage. Is this cruelty or a necessity if humans are to be fed?

may reduce the need to use antibiotics and chemicals (which can have bad side-effects on animals and humans alike).

FOR GOOD?...

Genetic modification has extended the very idea of agriculture. Animals can now be bred and 'farmed' to provide medicines for humans. At the Roslin Institute in Scotland, a flock of sheep have received a copy of a gene that makes a human protein called alpha-1-antitrypsin present in their milk. In this way, the protein can then be produced in large quantities and used in the treatment of painful lung diseases such as emphysema. The sheep themselves remain totally healthy.

...OR FOR BAD?

Breeding animals to develop certain qualities, such as increased weight or more milk, is as old as agriculture itself. However, some animal rights activists are concerned that genetic modification may lead to harmful changes as well. It is quite possible to breed animals of such high body weight that they cannot move easily or feed without help. Of course, this is true of traditional breeding methods. For example, the bulldog has been bred to have such deep folds of skin on its head that it suffers constantly from skin infections and other problems. But genetic modification linked to other demands for intensive farming will make such changes quicker and less easy to control.

Intensive farming

Agriculture in the developed world has become an industrialized '**agribusiness**'. The effects can be seen in the way animals are reared and fed, and this has led to many concerns about the welfare of farm animals.

'Factory farming'

Animal rights campaigners have highlighted the plight of chickens, pigs and veal calves, living in cramped cages, never seeing daylight, and dying from disease in huge numbers. They point to the practice of 'debeaking' birds to stop them pecking one another. The debeaking is a mechanized process which, it is argued, causes more pain to the birds. Campaigners see such treatment as cruel and unnecessary. If we must eat animal products, they say, then we should use less intensive methods that will allow farm animals to roam freely and live as naturally as possible. They find it unacceptable that many chickens live in crowded, unnatural environments, or that veal calves are fed an unnatural diet and raised in pens where they can hardly move.

Jill Phipps (left) – an animal rights campaigner killed in 1995 while protesting against the live export of veal calves.

THE FIVE FREEDOMS

The farming industry in Britain has taken many of the arguments against **intensive farming** seriously and the Farm Animal Welfare Council has drawn up Codes of Recommendation which ask farmers to be concerned for the health and welfare of animals. The Code is summarized in The Five Freedoms:

- Freedom from hunger
- Freedom from thirst
- Freedom from pain
- Freedom from fear
- Freedom of movement

CASE STUDY

Sid Jenkins, an RSPCA inspector, once followed a lorry loaded with sheep from Aberystwyth in Wales to Biggar in Scotland on a journey that lasted a total of thirty hours and fifteen minutes. During that time, although the driver had a good night's rest, the animals were not unloaded, or fed or watered. The law at the time said that animals must be fed after no more than twelve hours.

Keeping animals healthy

Farmers also recognize that only healthy animals can provide us with healthy food. However, there are many disagreements about how animals are best kept healthy. Animal welfare campaigners argue that healthy animals are those allowed to roam freely. Farmers and vets point out that all animals can have diseases. They say that while some diseases are made worse by intensive rearing, **free-range** living alone is not the answer. For instance, most outbreaks of salmonella, a disease that can lead to serious food-poisoning, have occurred in the eggs of free-range, not **battery-reared**, flocks of chickens.

However they are bred and reared, the time comes when many animals have to be transported to abattoirs (where they are killed) or to other farms. The conditions in which they are moved have also concerned animal welfare campaigners.

During the early 1990s other campaigners highlighted the stress caused to animals being transported from the UK into the rest of Europe. In 1993 over three million live animals were transported in this way. In the same year, Government rules were relaxed to allow journeys of fifteen hours in the UK and up to twenty-four hours in all, without food or water or a period outside the lorry. Activists blockaded seaports, and public opinion forced the main ferry companies to stop carrying live animals for a time. By 1995 new rules were in place and the trade began again, but the protests had been effective and now many fewer animals are involved.

HAMILTON COLLEGE LIBRARY

Vegetarianism

The treatment of animals in the chain of food production has led many people to believe that it is wrong to kill and eat animals. They have chosen to become **vegetarian**.

When the British Vegetarian Society was formed in 1847, it was about much more than not eating meat. 'Vegetarian' has nothing to do with 'vegetables', it comes from the Latin word *vegetus*, which means 'fresh' or 'whole'. To be a vegetarian was to pursue a whole and healthy lifestyle. Early vegetarians gave up meat because they believed we were not made to be meat-eaters, that it was unhealthy and unnatural.

It was only later, in the pioneering books by Henry Salt, *Animal Rights* and *A Plea for Vegetarianism* (1886), that vegetarianism began to be linked with compassion towards animals. It influenced both the great Indian leader Mahatma Gandhi and the playwright George Bernard Shaw, though it had little immediate impact. But it is this aspect that is now the dominant one. Modern vegetarians are most likely to echo Peter Singer's view in *Animal Liberation* that disgust at the way animals are treated in farms, abattoirs and factories has led them to vegetarianism.

Two famous vegetarians: Mahatma Gandhi (right) and George Bernard Shaw (opposite).

Modern vegetarianism is:
- *a response to what people think is the cruel treatment of animals*
- *a dislike of the idea of eating animals at all*
- *a recognition that more of the world's resources are used in producing meat than in growing plants for food*

VEGANISM

Another recent development is veganism. Vegetarians give up *animal flesh*. Vegans reject all *animal products*, including fish, eggs, cheese and butter.

Healthy eating

Many people become vegetarian or even vegan at some time in their lives, and we

certainly now know the importance of eating a lot of fruit and vegetables for good health. It is quite possible to eat a nutritious diet without ever touching meat. It is possible, though harder, to do so without eating any animal products, as vegans demand. Other people choose only to eat meat from wild animals or fish. Yet others will only eat meat that is 'organic' – from **free-range** farms that do not use pesticides, chemical fertilizers or antibiotics. For some it is a matter of like and dislike, for others a **moral** position. Some reject meat because they are horrified by the processes of farming. Others believe, with the 18th century French philosopher Jean-Jacques Rousseau and the founders of vegetarianism, that it is unnatural for humans to eat animal flesh and that, for good health, we should only eat fruit and vegetables. What do you think?

The politics of food

Bovine spongiform encephalopathy (BSE)

BSE is a disease first identified in cattle in 1986, which has particularly affected the British Isles. The epidemic reached its peak in 1992 and in 13 years there have been over 175,000 cases, although the numbers of infected animals have now declined considerably. BSE was caused by the practice of feeding animal protein to other animals. This happened all over the world but for various reasons the effects were particularly bad in the United Kingdom and led to a long-lasting ban on the export of beef, and widespread slaughter of cattle. BSE might be the cause of a debilitating brain disease called Creuzfeldt-Jacob Disease (CJD) in some humans, although this is not certain. The whole story of BSE, its causes and effects, illustrates the way in which animals become caught up in what is called the **politics of food**.

Food and power

It has been said that 'the one who controls food, controls the world'. It could also be said that our attitude to the way in which our food is produced is a clear indication of our attitude to the world around us. Campaigners remind us of the cost in animal suffering of our need for food. They ask us to consider whether our need for food justifies the way we breed, rear, transport and then kill animals. They ask us to consider whether we need to eat animals and animal products at all.

We all have to eat. Nourishing food is essential to life. Food can also give us

Despite assurances from the Minister of Agriculture that beef was safe to eat, British beef exports were banned in the BSE crisis.

great pleasure. It is right to be thankful for our food. But we do not have to think about food for very long before we begin to realize that it raises plenty of **moral** questions too. There are the questions about how our food is produced, and we have been raising some of these in this book. But there are other questions too.

From the farm to the table

Many people in developed societies, living in towns and buying food from supermarkets, forget the chain of events that leads to a meal on the table.

Farming and food production is a skilled process. There is enough food in the world for everyone, but political and economic factors play a part in its distribution. The cost and availability of food can make a difference between life and death, nourishment and starvation. Some methods of food production may not be safe – food may become infected or cause other diseases in humans. There are good arguments for not having battery-reared chickens, but what if this is the only method that will produce enough eggs to feed everyone at a price they can afford? The mass production of food involves mechanized killing processes, but what if this is the only way in which enough food can be distributed quickly and widely to everyone who wants or needs it?

There is enough food to feed the world, but while developed nations overproduce food, many countries are regularly caught in the grip of famine.

Complex issues

Campaigners remind us of the conditions in which we keep and kill the animals we eat, or whose products we use – from feathers in our duvets to milk on our breakfast cereal. These conditions are often stressful, and animals can be subjected to many cruelties in the pursuit of profit. But we also have a duty to feed the hungry. In the end we cannot separate how we treat animals from how we treat each other.

The environment and wild animals

Animal rights are about the way we take responsible decisions for ourselves and the great diversity of life with which we share our planet. We as human beings differ from other living creatures in our ability to change the world around us. What do we do with that power? One way is to see the world as a place to be conquered. In this view, human wishes and needs are the most important consideration, and the natural world is simply there to be made use of. We have seen how thinkers such as Henry Salt and Tom Regan disagree with that view. For them, animals are individuals in their own right, to be respected, enjoyed and allowed to live for themselves and in their own way. Animals are not there for what we can get out of them.

'In Wildness is the preservation of the World'. This painting by Albert Bierstadt shows the Yosemite Valley in California in 1868, soon to become the first national park in America.

The other way is to see the world as a place in need of our care and protection as guardians or stewards. In this view, our ability to reflect on the world around us, to understand it, and to change it, should be focused on 'making the world make itself', loving it for what it is.

The world of television

For so many people, the natural world is only seen in programmes on television. It is a far-away world, brought to us through sensitive filming and skilful commentaries. It is easy for programmes like these to reinforce the idea that humans are the most important form of life on the planet. We can look on these strange and wonderful birds, mammals, fish or insects as being there simply for our entertainment. We lose sight of the delicate balance of nature – the **biodiversity** that makes every species reliant on others. And we also easily forget that our own interests – for food, shelter, transport and power – have an impact on the world around us, which can upset this delicate balance in a frighteningly short time.

The first national park

In 1846 Henry David Thoreau walked near Mount Ktaadn in Maine in the eastern United States. He later described the place: 'Here was no man's garden... It was vast, terrific [terrifying].' Yet this sense of awe and terror became for Thoreau a necessary part of our relationship to the world. He said some time later, 'in Wildness is the preservation of the World.' Since Thoreau's time, many others have shared the same experience. One was John Muir, who later in the 19th century walked in the great forests and mountains of California and fought to have them preserved as the Yosemite National Park, the first of its kind in the world.

FOUNDERS OF CONSERVATION

Henry Thoreau and John Muir were the founders of an environmental movement in which humans take responsibility for preserving and maintaining wild places, and fight for the rights of animals to live there undisturbed.

Both men had a love of the natural world around them; they were bowled over by its beauty. Their awe and reverence deepened over time into a passionate protectiveness for the environment, not only for its own sake but also for the way the natural world could remind humans of great truths, as they saw it, of the mystery and majesty of creation.

Henry David Thoreau developed a love for nature which deepened into protectiveness.

27

Zoos

The first elephant arrived in England in 1254, a present to King Henry III from the King of France. It was kept in the royal **menagerie** at the Tower of London, and visitors had to pay to see it. The Tower was not the first place in England to have exotic animals. One hundred and fifty years earlier, King Henry I had a menagerie at Woodstock near Oxford where he kept lions, lynxes, leopards and camels. Exotic animal keeping was essentially a royal practice – in ancient Egypt and China, and in medieval England and Europe. But after the French Revolution, in 1792, the remaining animals in the king's zoo at Versailles formed the basis of a new public menagerie in Paris.

At the same time in England there was a travelling menagerie owned by George Pidcock, based in London, which included a kangaroo and a boa constrictor.

Great architecture but cruel environment? The elephant house at London Zoo.

FACT

● *In 1826 the Zoological Society of London was founded and its gardens in Regent's Park were soon open to the public. In 1867 the full title of the gardens was shortened in a popular song, and the word 'zoo' was born.*

Zoos and animal rights

Henry Salt, in his book *Animal Rights*, was one of the first to protest against shutting up animals in cages. His distaste for the idea was based partly on the restrictive environment and partly on the way animals in zoos 'lose their character'. This two-pronged attack on the unnatural environment of zoos has been the focus of objections ever since.

Zoos have themselves gradually responded to these criticisms, and in many cases changed the way they keep animals. The often cramped conditions of town-based zoos have given way to open environments, such as Whipsnade Zoo in England, and safari parks. At the same time, national parks in such countries as Australia, America, Africa and India have made it possible to see animals in a more natural environment.

Endangered species

The Jardin des Plantes in Paris and the London Zoological Society's gardens were founded partly for the scientific study of animals. In recent decades, this has developed into a concern for **conservation** and breeding of **endangered species**, and their return to the wild. Zoos claim some success in this, although animal welfare campaigners have argued that the actual numbers of species saved, or animals returned to the wild, are far too low to justify the conditions in which they are kept. Animal campaigners have also attacked zoos for their record in collecting animals from the wild. Indeed the traffic in wild animals, not just to stock zoos and provide pets but also for trade in ivory (elephant tusks) and skins, has been condemned as a source of needless suffering that depends on human vanity and greed.

Some zoos, such as the one in Jersey, founded by Gerald Durrell, emphasize the importance of conservation and breeding rare species to release back into the wild.

Gerald Durrell

Animal conservationists argue that removing some endangered species from environments where they are at risk is necessary if they are to survive in the long term. The work of the late Gerald Durrell at the Jersey Wildlife Preservation Trust, popularized in his many books, is perhaps the most famous argument for the role of zoos in conservation.

The work of the Jersey Wildlife Preservation Trust shows also that zoos have an important educational function. They enable people to see real animals, and understand something of their behaviour and their beauty, in much more direct ways than television documentaries. But this too can only be justified if all zoos reach the standard of the best ones, with strict controls to prevent cruelty and exploitation.

The circus

No one knows who first taught an animal to perform tricks to make others laugh or be amazed. There is little doubt, though, that travelling players have often done just that. The first modern circus was begun by Philip Astley in London in 1768. At first, Astley's circus used only horses, running inside a ring or circle ('circus' comes from the Greek word *kirkos*, meaning a ring). But he quickly added clowns, acrobats and other performers. In 1783 Astley opened another circus in Paris and soon circuses were all the rage in Europe and also in America, where John Ricketts started a show in 1793.

Travelling shows

During the 19th and 20th centuries circuses added more and more acts, and began to tour, performing in huge tents (big tops). They took all their human and animal acts with them, travelling in caravans and cages. In England, circus families, such as Billy Smart and the Chipperfields, became famous and popular entertainers. The shows included a range of performing animals, trained to do a wide variety of tricks. Astley's use of animals quickly expanded from just horses to include lions and tigers, elephants, seals and dogs as well.

Performing horses – some of the earliest traditional circus acts.

> ### FACT
>
> ● *As early as 1911 an English law was passed (the Protection of Animals Act) to protect circus animals from cruelty and suffering.*

Animal-free circuses

Gradually, public opinion swung against animal acts. The training was thought to be cruel, and making animals perform both cruel and degrading. In addition, people came to believe that the travelling to which the animals were subjected as the circus moved from place to place was

Cirque du Soleil – one of the many modern circuses that refuse to use animal acts.

likely to make them suffer. Nowadays, many circuses are deliberately animal-free. In Britain, Circus Hassini put into effect the ambition of the famous clown Coco to see a circus based on human skill alone. Other internationally famous companies, such as the French Cirque du Soleil and the Australian Circus Oz, have shown that circuses can still be wonderful entertainment without any performing animals at all.

What do you think?

Some circuses continue to use animals. They accept that there has been abuse in the past but argue that animals will only perform if they love and trust their trainer, something that does not come from ill-treatment or fear. They argue that most trainers want their animals to be happy and healthy. Animals, they say, perform because they want to.

Against this, animal welfare groups argue that there can be no good reason for circuses to have animal acts. They point out that there have been many cases of circus owners and animal trainers being prosecuted for cruelty. Even the most careful trainer cannot prevent the unnecessary suffering caused to animals by their training, performances, and especially their confinement in cages and travelling from place to place. Many towns and cities no longer allow circuses with animal acts to perform on their land.

FACT

● *Dolphins and whales are remarkably intelligent creatures. They too can learn tricks and have been kept in confinement in marinas – circuses with water – to be trained and perform. From 1987 an active campaign was launched to have marinas and similar places closed down. By 1993 the last British marine park had closed down and dolphins and whales were being increasingly returned to the wild.*

Hunting

The hunt – one of the traditional images of 'Olde England'. Sport or barbarity?

Field sport or blood sport? For many people the question of whether or not hunting should be banned is a very emotional one. For some, it is a key part of the country scene, a sport with many practical and economic uses. For others, it is a barbaric and cruel practice in which animals – usually foxes and stags, but also sometimes hares – are chased until, terrified and exhausted, they are caught and killed by packs of dogs. When, in 1999, the British government announced that it would bring in a law to ban hunting using dogs, opinion was **polarized** once more.

Field sport?...

Those who argue that hunting should not be banned make four main points. First of all, they say that hunting is of economic importance to the life of the countryside. Many people are employed to breed and look after the horses and dogs used in hunting. It also helps to conserve the land. A landscape used for hunting, they say, has more hedges and coppices and maintains a more varied wildlife than one in which hunting has ended. Second, the fox is a pest and its numbers need to be kept down to maintain wildlife, as well as chickens, geese and ducks on farms. The alternative method of killing foxes by shooting them is no less cruel. Third, they say that hunting is a traditional and enjoyable sport and those who wish to pursue it should be allowed to. Hunting is a minority sport, but really no less cruel than fishing, and the government is not proposing to ban fishing. Finally they argue that opponents of hunting are people who live in towns, who do not understand the ways of the country. Town-dwellers have not grasped the economic necessities, or the place of hunting in rural life. They are just sentimental about foxes.

...Or blood sport?

Those who argue that hunting should be banned disagree with each of these points. They argue that employment and conservation in the countryside can be managed without hunting. Indeed, they say, those in favour of hunting are often precisely those who oppose developing rural economies through small industries, but who also condone destroying hedges and using pesticides to increase farmers' profits. Everyone agrees that the fox is a pest, but those against hunting argue that foxes can be shot, a more humane death than being attacked by dogs. And what about the stag and the hare, which are also hunted, but are not pests? (Hares are in fact becoming an **endangered species** in Britain.) Finally, they say that it is simply not true that only town-dwellers oppose hunting, many farmers do too, not least because of the damage hunting causes to their land and crops.

What do you think?

Both sides agree that fox and stag hunting and hare-coursing are cruel. Hunted animals do suffer. Where they disagree is on whether the cruelty is justified by the outcome. Most of us probably would not agree with the British Member of Parliament who is alleged to have said of hunting, 'Of course it's cruel, but I enjoy it.' But what about the other arguments? Is hunting so important to rural economy, or employment, that it needs to continue? Is it the best way to manage the fox population? (But what about stags and hares?) Are opponents of hunting just sentimentalists who neither understand nor tolerate the ways of the country? How different is hunting a fox with dogs from catching a fish on a barbed hook and dragging it to land, exhausted and suffocating? What do you think?

Hunt saboteurs at work, watched by police. While many ways of sabotaging the hunt are not illegal, violence can erupt between the two sides.

Working animals

Dogs

Dogs were the first wild creatures to be **domesticated**. More than 12,000 years ago they were probably being used as hunting animals and then as guard dogs. Wild dogs are pack animals – like the wolf – and adopt the humans with whom they live as their 'family'. A relationship of trust can grow up in which dog and human share in the gathering of food and mutual protection. Dogs' instincts for hunting in a group can be developed and used not only for hunting but also for gathering sheep. So the hunting dog and the sheepdog use the same behaviour, modified by training and breeding, to meet human needs.

More recently the same instinctive relationships have been used to train dogs to act as guide dogs for the blind and visually impaired, and as hearing dogs for the deaf. Dogs are also trained for rescue – for example, the famous Saint Bernard dogs used in the mountains of Europe. Their highly-developed sense of smell has meant they can follow a trail in conditions and over distances that would defeat most people, and help find people buried in avalanches. The same ability to follow a scent makes dogs valuable in police work as well – as sniffer dogs for drugs or explosives. Dogs are also used for sport, not just in hunting, but also in racing.

Sheepdogs at work. Many breeds of dog have become important partners to humans.

GREYHOUND RESCUE

This is Billy. He spent three months scavenging for food in a wood before he was caught and taken to a rescue centre. He was very thin, covered in cuts and scars, and very scared. He had been beaten severely, then abandoned. But Billy is one of the lucky ones. Today he lives in a loving home with two other dogs. Each year, thousands of greyhounds like Billy are abandoned when their racing days are over, at four years old or younger. Many are put down, and many are sent abroad for **vivisection**. Some end up in rescue centres, but others are less fortunate. Greyhounds have been found hanging from trees, abandoned with their muzzles on so that they cannot eat, or, worse still, wrapped in barbed wire and left to die. And all because they no longer make any money for their owners.

Horses

The dog was the first animal to be domesticated, followed by sheep and cattle, for food, and by oxen, to pull ploughs and carts. About 5000 years ago, in the Middle East and Central Asia, people began to use small wild horses to pull light carts. As they were bred to be bigger and stronger, so, perhaps 4000 years ago, humans learned to ride, bringing about one of the most significant changes in civilization. Horse and rider together became a powerful, terrifying weapon, and the cavalry dominated warfare until early in the 20th century.

The horse, then, has been both a symbol of peace – even today, rural life is typified by the horse and cart and the horse-drawn plough – and of war and domination. With the growth of steam, petrol and electric power, the practical use of the horse has declined, but it still stirs strong emotions in us. For many people, horse-riding is a much-loved childhood experience, and many continue to ride for pleasure all their lives. This is another example of the horse as a

Mongol cavalry, from a 14th century Arabic history book.

symbol of peace. But the memory of the warrior on horseback lingers on in the sport of horse-racing, where specially bred and trained animals gallop at speed, often over jumps.

Animal welfare campaigners have criticized horse-racing both for the danger to the animals during racing and the suffering caused them during breeding and training. Those involved with horses, however, while accepting the risks, deny that breeding and training causes suffering. They point out that because these horses are valuable they are well cared for, and that jockeys as well as horses are at risk in races.

But, while jockeys know the risks they run, horses do not. They gallop and jump by instinct developed through training. There is no real sense in which we could say that horses 'agree' to do what they do. What sort of responsibility do humans have to protect animals, with whom they share their life and work, from suffering?

Animal welfare organizations

The 19th century was a time of social reform. Slavery was abolished, child labour in factories controlled, living conditions improved, hospitals and schools opened. At the same time, and as part of the aim to make people more **morally** aware and responsible, laws began to be passed to prevent cruelty to animals. In 1809, the Society for the Suppression and Prevention of Wanton Cruelty to Animals was started in Liverpool. In 1822 the Animal Protection Act was passed in parliament and, in 1824, the Society for the Prevention of Cruelty to Animals (SPCA) was founded at a meeting in Old Slaughter's Coffee House in London. Sixteen years later the SPCA received royal approval and was renamed RSPCA – the Royal Society for the Prevention of Cruelty to Animals.

The RSPCA

From its beginnings, the RSPCA has had two roles. First, to educate people not to treat animals cruelly, and second, to act as a police force to prevent cruelty and prosecute anyone found ill-treating animals. In 1832 the SPCA employed two inspectors (then called constables); the number had risen to eighty by 1855. In 1856 the constables were given uniforms very like those worn by the police.

Portrait of Richard Martin, MP, one of the founders of the SPCA, the forerunner of the RSPCA.

FACTS

- *Today, the RSPCA has over 300 inspectors who investigate more than 100,000 complaints every year.*
- *In addition to its education and protection work, the RSPCA has animal hospitals in England and Wales that treat more than a quarter of a million creatures every year.*

The RSPCA has played a key role in animal welfare in Britain for more than 150 years. It is concerned about cruelty to all creatures, from farm animals to pet birds, from racehorses to badgers. It has also been active in arguing for the introduction of new laws to protect different groups of animals and birds.

The RSPCA in England was the first of many animal welfare organizations throughout the world. During the 20th century, others, such as the World Wildlife Fund and the Born Free Foundation, were founded. You will find more information about these at the end of this book.

Animal law

Since the first Animal Protection Act sponsored by Richard Martin in 1822, many other laws have been passed in the UK concerning the treatment of animals. One is the Performing Animals Act of 1925, which requires animal trainers and exhibitors to be licensed and allows the police to enter premises to check on the animals. Another is the Wildlife and Countryside Act of 1981, with its emphasis on **conservation** and international law governing the catching and transportation of wild animals and birds.

In fact, animal law is now a vast and complicated area of work for lawyers. There are laws about animal welfare and cruelty; animals being used for scientific purposes; wild animals, farm animals and pets, and even about how whales stranded on beaches should be protected from souvenir hunters.

Animal welfare in Britain is controlled by law and policed by the RSPCA. However, a complex structure of government inspection and administration has also been set up, as seen in, for instance, the Animals (Scientific Procedures) Act of 1986, which deals with **vivisection**.

To this extent, the question of whether or not animals have 'rights' has been answered. The many laws governing the treatment of animals mean that we have a legal responsibility to treat other living creatures in such a way that we do not cause them unnecessary suffering. In that sense, at least, they have a 'right' to be treated well by us.

PROTECTION – UP TO A POINT

The Wildlife and Countryside Act (1981) protects all animals living in the wild. It also makes it illegal to release species of animals into the wild which are not native to Britain. However, the act makes it possible for people to obtain a licence to capture or kill wild animals for particular purposes – for instance, for scientific research.

Living with animals

We share our planet with millions of other species of living things. Animal rights are about how we take responsible decisions for our own lives and behaviour and for all the other creatures around us. Animals cannot themselves demand rights – only human beings have that capacity – but we can give them the opportunity to live freely, to share their lives with us without cruelty and unnecessary suffering.

For some people that will mean deciding not to eat meat, and possibly other animal products. It may involve campaigning against animal experiments,

Humans share their lives with animals in many different ways. We have a legal duty not to cause them unnecessary suffering.

or zoos, or circuses, or hunting. Other people may carry on eating meat, but want to be sure that the way animals are bred, reared, transported and killed does not cause them unnecessary distress.

Some people will make these decisions because, like Henry Salt and Tom Regan, they believe that animals should be treated as individuals, with the same sort of compassion and justice we would show to one another. Others will want, like Peter Singer, to weigh up the balance of suffering with the positive outcome that may result – for instance, whether infecting mice with cancer cells can be justified by the cure for cancer that such research may lead to – and make their decisions on that basis.

But we must make each of these decisions for ourselves. First we should gather as many facts as possible about issues that concern us. Then we have to do some hard thinking. **Moral** decisions about how we ought to treat animals can be informed by facts, but in the end they are based on something else. They depend on how we think humans should behave.

from predators. As with the hunting of foxes, we may need to kill in order to keep the balance right. But morally, too, there are decisions to be made. What sort of people do we want to be? Dominators or sharers? Rulers or co-operators? We may need to kill animals – for food, or for our own or other species' protection. The moral question will then be, how do we do that killing? Is it all right to kill, and enjoy it as a sport? Our attitude to animal rights will depend in the end on our answers to questions like these.

The freedom of other species to live freely on our planet can be destroyed more easily than we might imagine.

WHAT IS OUR ROLE?

Are we 'the lords of nature'? Is it our own survival and well-being that matters? Is the world around us only there to be used for our own needs? Or are we guardians of nature? Does our survival really depend on the well-being of the world around us? Do all living creatures have their own value, separate from us? Are they precious just because they are alive?

Keeping the right balance

The questions are both practical and moral. The delicate balance of nature can be upset more easily by human action than by anything else (except perhaps collision with a comet). Our own survival may depend on maintaining a rich diversity of life – from the school hedge to the rainforests of the Amazon. It may depend, too, on working within the natural order to protect some species

What can I do?

How we should treat animals is an important and complicated matter. It raises questions about science and politics, agriculture (factory farming) and entertainment (zoos and circuses), and the economics of country life. Campaigners for animal welfare will often see their concerns as embracing not just the treatment of animals, but also what they, the human campaigners, should eat and wear. Not so long ago, it was not unusual for people to wear clothes made from animal fur. Today, fewer people wear them and campaigners have succeeded in closing down many farms that bred animals for the fur trade. The opponents of **intensive breeding** and rearing of animals are often so horrified by what they believe to be the cruelty of this practice, that they become **vegetarians** or **vegans** and refuse to eat animals or animal products.

Legal protest

These examples show how beliefs about the right treatment of animals have an impact on daily life. You may decide to change what you do, what you eat or

Publicizing cases of cruelty has always been one of the most effective deterrents.

what you wear. But you might go further than that. For example, you might decide that it is wrong to go to a circus that uses performing animals. But, if such a circus came to your town, you could express your views by writing a letter of protest to the local council to try to get them to change their policy. You could also be active in trying to persuade your family or friends not to go. There are many lawful ways you can make your feelings known.

In the same way, you may decide you only want to use cosmetics, toiletries or household products that have not been tested on animals. Sometimes you can find this out by looking on the labels, but that is not always fool-proof. You may decide you need to write to the manufacturer and ask them for their policy on animal testing, and a list of products that have not been tested on animals at any stage in their making. If you are not happy about their answers, you may decide not to use that manufacturer's products. You may even try to persuade your friends not to use them either.

Some people who are concerned about animal welfare take a very different approach. For example, you may dislike factory farming methods but not want to give up meat or chicken. The law usually describes cruelty to animals as actions that cause 'unnecessary suffering'. So, once again, you may decide to contact the manufacturer and ask for their policy on animal welfare before you decide to buy what they are offering. Your family may be able to find organic producers, or local farmers and firms where you can see how their animals are cared for.

PRESSURE GROUPS

Many people find that they can bring about changes by working with others who agree with them. In this way they can share ideas, and their point of view can have a bigger impact on the public. If you feel strongly about some of the things discussed in this book, you and some of your friends could get together to learn more about them, and perhaps to find ways in which you can tell other people about your concerns. So long as you stay within the bounds of what is legal, you might even try to change things, or at least change other people's attitude to them.

Taking responsibility

These examples show one other important point. Animal rights are about how you believe animals should be treated. They say as much about you as about the animals themselves. How do you want to treat the whole world around you? There are many things that people who are concerned about animal welfare can do. But the best results come when we start to change ourselves and think about how we want to live, taking responsibility for our own thoughts and actions. Animal rights are not just about farm animals, or foxes, or scientific experiments, important though these things are. They are also, for instance, about how we treat our own pets, or the wildlife we see in the countryside or in parks and gardens. It takes people to be cruel, and people to be caring. Animal rights are above all about human responsibility.

Where can I find out more?

Some of the best and most up-to-date information about animal rights issues can be found on the Internet. As for all popular topics, there is an enormous number of websites to explore. One search engine gives over 46,000 websites on the topic of 'animal rights' alone. Browsing through these sites can take a long time. And beware! – a lot of strong feelings get expressed on the Internet, and there can be some very distressing pictures and descriptions. Try **www.orbyss.com/animl1.htm** for a list of sites for named animal rights organizations.

Most of the organizations in this section have publications and projects of particular interest to young people. Their postal addresses, telephone numbers and website addresses are given on the 'Contacts' page of this book (page 46). Public libraries and your school library will probably have more information, especially on local organizations or branches of the national societies close to you.

FARM ANIMALS

Compassion in World Farming is an animal welfare organization that campaigns on many issues to do with the breeding, rearing, transporting and slaughtering of animals. Contact the Country Landowners Association for information on the farmers' side of the argument.

RSPCA

The Royal Society for the Prevention of Cruelty to Animals (RSPCA) is the oldest animal welfare organization. You will find they have a great deal of useful information on a variety of topics, with ideas about how you can help them in their work.

BIRDS AND DOGS

If your particular interest is birds, then contact the Royal Society for the Protection of Birds (RSPB). For everything to do with the training and placement of guide dogs, contact the Guidedogs for the Blind Association. The Tia Greyhound Rescue finds and re-homes abandoned greyhounds and lurchers. In the three years that Tia has been running, it has found homes for more than 200 dogs.

WILD ANIMALS AND CIRCUSES

The Born Free Foundation is an action group inspired by the book and film of the same name. Its 'Magnificent 7' Projects are committed to protecting and conserving **endangered species**, and wherever possible enabling them to live in their wild state. One of its projects is dedicated to protecting dolphins and whales. Another campaigns against the use of animals in circuses. For the other side of the circus picture, you could look up the Circus Animals Care and Training website.

WILDLIFE TRADE

The worldwide traffic in capturing wild animals, transporting them from country to country and selling them for profit has led to many concerns. TRAFFIC, a branch of the World Wildlife Fund, monitors the often cruel wildlife trade and highlights the importance of keeping it within the bounds of international law.

ZOO CONSERVATION

The Jersey Wildlife Preservation Trust shows how **conservation** programmes within the environment of a zoo can be beneficial to endangered species and educational at the same time.

CONSERVATION – WORLDWIDE

This book has argued that animal rights concerns only make sense in the context of wider conservation issues. How we treat animals is just one part of our attitude to the world around us. The first environmental organization was the International Union for the Conservation of Nature and Natural Resources (IUCN), created in 1948. It publishes information about endangered wildlife in its Red Data Book. Other famous international organizations are Greenpeace, the World Wildlife Fund and Friends of the Earth. Their publications and websites are packed with interesting and useful information.

CONSERVATION – UK

The Wildlife Trusts are the main focus for conservation matters in the United Kingdom. Contact your local branch for information on activities in your area.

The earth seen from the moon. Environmentalists remind us how fragile is the balance of nature and how great is our responsibility to care for the planet on which we live.

Glossary

agribusiness the whole world of farming and food production, from the supply of farm machinery to the distribution of crops and livestock to factories or markets

apartheid a political system which deliberately keeps different races separate

battery-reared an animal bred and brought up in small cages or compounds, artificially and quickly fattened for market or made to produce eggs

biodiversity the recognition that life on our planet is made up of many different species, dependent on one another for survival

civil rights movement political organizations committed to establishing human rights

conservation preserving the natural world – plants and animals – for the future

discrimination treating another person or thing as having fewer rights or less value simply because they are different

domesticated a once wild animal (or species of animal) now tamed to help humans, or provide food – for example, dogs and cats, horses, cattle and sheep

Draize a type of animal experimentation, named after its inventor, John Draize

emancipation the freeing of slaves

endangered species animals that are close to extinction often as a result of human activities

environmentally friendly a phrase used to describe those manufactured goods which are unlikely to badly affect the world around us

free-range originally used to describe eggs laid by chickens allowed to roam freely in the open, rather than being kept confined to small cages; now also used to describe any animal or bird being farmed in these outdoor conditions

genetic code the way in which our genes (the building blocks of life that determine our characteristics) pass on their information from parent to child

Green the political movement concerned with environmental issues. The word is also used to express a general attitude about the care of the environment

intensive farming using (often artificial) methods to get the highest levels of production or yield from crops or livestock

interdependence the need of different individuals or species for one another

menagerie a collection of wild animals; the original name for a zoo, now sometimes used as an alternative

moral a term used to describe behaviour that is generally regarded by a community as good and right

oppression preventing people from living freely

stimuli plural for 'stimulus' – anything that provokes a response in a living organism

symbiotic a term describing a relationship between two individuals or two species that is mutually helpful

theory of evolution the account of how higher and more complex species have gradually evolved from simpler organisms over millions of years, that was first developed by Charles Darwin (1809–82)

tranquillizer a type of drug, used to calm anxieties or relax a person

vegetarianism eating only vegetable products, not animals, out of personal preference or moral belief

vivisection experiments which involve surgically operating on living creatures

Contacts and helplines

BORN FREE FOUNDATION
3 Grove House, Foundry Land
Horsham, West Sussex RH13 5PL
01403 240170 – www.bornfree.org.uk

CIRCUS ANIMALS TRAINING AND CARE
www.firstlight.net/~animals

COMPASSION IN WORLD FARMING
Charles House, 5A Charles Street
Petersfield, Hampshire GU32 3EH
01730 264208/268863 – www.ciwf.co.uk

COUNTRY LANDOWNERS ASSOCIATION
16 Belgrave Square London, SW1X 8PQ
020 7235 0511 – www.cla.org.uk

FRIENDS OF THE EARTH
26-28 Underwood Street, London, N1 7JQ
020 7490 0881 – www.foe.co.uk

GREENPEACE
Canonbury Villas, London, N1 2PN
020 7354 5100 – www.greenpeace.org

GUIDEDOGS FOR THE BLIND ASSOCIATION
Hillfields, Burghfield Common,
Reading RG7 3YG
0118 983 5555 – www.gdba.org.uk

INTERNATIONAL FUND FOR ANIMAL WELFARE
Warren Court, Park Road
Crowborough, East Sussex TN6 2GA
01892 601 900 – www.ifaw.org

INTERNATIONAL WILDLIFE COALITION
141A High Street, Edenbridge
Kent TN6 5AX
01732 666955
www.webcom.com/iwcwww

IUCN
219c Huntingdon Road
Cambridge CB3 0DL
01223 277 894 – iucn.org

JERSEY WILDLIFE PRESERVATION TRUST
Les Augrés Manor, Trinity
Jersey JE3 5BP
01534 860000 – www.durrell.org/zoo

ROYAL SOCIETY FOR THE PREVENTION OF CRUELTY TO ANIMALS (RSPCA)
Enquiries: Causeway, Horsham
West Sussex RH12 1HG
0870 444 3127
Cruelty Hotline: *0870 5555 999*
www.rspca.co.uk

ROYAL SOCIETY FOR THE PROTECTION OF BIRDS (RSPB)
The Lodge, Sandy, Bedfordshire SG19 2DL
01767 680551 – www.rspb.org.uk

TIA GREYHOUND RESCUE
Sowerby Bridge, West Yorkshire
01422 884062 or *01943 816790*

THE WILDLIFE TRUSTS
(National Office) The Kiln, Waterside,
Mather Road, Newark, Notts NG24 1WT
01636 677711 – wildlifetrust.org.uk

WORLD WILDLIFE FUND
Panda House, Weyside Park, Godalming,
Surrey GU7 1XR
01483 426 444 – www.wwf-uk.org

IN AUSTRALIA

GREENPEACE AUSTRALIA-PACIFIC
Level 4, 35-39 Liverpool Street
Sydney, NSW 2000
2 9261 4666 – www.greenpeace.org

Further reading

Fiction

A Zoo in My Luggage
Gerald Durrell
Penguin, 1970

Encounters with Animals
Gerald Durrell
Penguin, 1969

My Family and Other Animals
Gerald Durrell
Penguin, 1999

Non-fiction

An Unnatural Order: Why We Are Destroying the Planet and Each Other
Jim Mason
Continuum, 1997
This is not an easy read, but it is one of the best accounts of this topic that there has ever been.

Diet for a Gentle World: Eating with Conscience
Les Inglis
Avery, 1993

The Gaia Atlas of Planet Management
Norman Myers and Gerald Durrell
Gaia Books, 1994

How to be Animal Friendly: Choose the Kindest Ways to Eat, Shop and Have Fun
P Perry, C Grimshaw, P Mounter
Element, 1999

John Muir
S Tolan
Morehouse, 1990
People who Have Helped the World series

Index

HAMILTON COLLEGE LIBRARY